CREATED FOR

Greater Things

CREATED FOR
Greater Things

MOTHER TERESA'S
LIFE AND WITNESS

WITH A COMMENTARY BY
GLORIA HUTCHINSON

New City Press
Hyde Park, New York

Published in the United States by New City Press
202 Cardinal Rd., Hyde Park, NY 12538
www.newcitypress.com

Cover design by Durva Correia

Library of Congress Cataloging-in-Publication Data:

A copy of the CIP data is available from the Library of Congress.

ISBN 978-1-56548-285-2 (pbk. : alk. paper)

Printed in the United States of America

Contents

Introduction

Created for Greater Things

For we are what he has made us, created in Christ Jesus for good works, which God prepared beforehand to be our way of life.

Ephesians 2:10

God has created us for greater things: to love and be loved.

Mother Teresa

Mother Teresa as a young woman

To all who knew her, personally or through the media, Mother Teresa of Calcutta embodied Jesus' promise, "Truly I tell you, just as you did it to one of the least of these who are members of my family, you did it to me" (Mt 25:40). The works of mercy were her daily bread: feeding the hungry, giving drink to the thirsty, clothing the naked, sheltering the homeless, caring for and consoling the dying.

One by one the poorest of the poor received the compassionate tending of Mother Teresa and her Missionaries of Charity around the world. As Cardinal Angelo Sodano observed at her funeral on September 13, 1997, Mother Teresa taught the world a lesson it needed to hear: "It is more blessed to give than to receive" (Acts 20:35).

This woman who her contemporaries recognized as a saint understood the purpose of a human life. She knew that each person, as Paul writes, is "God's handiwork." We have been created in Christ to do the good works of the coming kingdom. Mother Teresa paid attention to those words. She put it this way

> We have not come into this
> world just to be a number ...
> We are children of God.
> We have been created for a
> purpose, for greater things:
> to love and to be loved.

She understood that people everywhere hunger for God, hunger for Jesus. Although they cannot see Jesus in person, they can experience his presence in those who care for them with a measure of his love.

> We all want to love God. But how can we love God whom we don't see. And so God made it possible for us to put our love for Him in a living action.

Unlike those often distracted by overwork, anxiety, or saturation in the media, Mother Teresa focused on a single goal. Each new day brought another opportunity to remain close to Christ through prayer and worship, and to serve him in his forgotten ones. It was a time to grow in his image:

> Just as the seed is meant to be a tree, we are meant to grow into Jesus.

Here is the key to Mother Teresa's spirituality: to be Christ for others, to see Christ in others — particularly those who, as she said, "have no one to call their own." It is a goal worthy of and demanding of a lifetime. A tree does not spring up overnight, nor does a saint. Happily, there is always nourishment available for the asking. Mother Teresa observed:

> Jesus made Himself the Bread
> of Life, that we may be able to
> eat and live and be able to see
> Him in the distressing disguise
> of the poor.

We were created for greater things. And the true definition of greatness belongs not to the world but to God himself. He alone measures the worth of our good works for Christ disguised as the poorest of the poor in our respective worlds.

> To show great love for God and
> our neighbor we need not do
> great things. It is how much love
> we put in the doing that makes
> our offering something beautiful
> for God.

Part 1

Life in Jesus Christ

The woman who the world came to know as Mother Teresa of Calcutta was born on August 26, 1910 in Skopje, Macedonia to Albanian Catholic parents. As a child, Gonxha (Agnes) Bojaxhiu lived in comfort. Yet she envisioned herself one day going to India to serve as a missionary. At eighteen she joined the Loreto Sisters of Dublin primarily because they had a mission station in Bengal. Her move to Ireland took her to a land where few understood her native tongue. Her Sisters recalled her as a quiet, shy, and ordinary novice.

When she made her first vows, young Gonxha took the name of Teresa to honor Thérèse of Lisieux. In 1931 she was sent to Entally, a district of Calcutta, to teach at St. Mary's School.

For the next fifteen years, Sr. Teresa taught history and geography to daughters of the wealthy. Her life was once again comfortable and secure. Living in obedience to her religious vows, Teresa was happy with her community and her students.

She might well have spent the rest of her years serving God and the church as an educator. But if she had, we would have lost the wisdom and witness of Blessed Mother Teresa of Calcutta and the world would have been a much poorer place.

Part I of this volume, which presents Mother Teresa's guidance on how to live as true followers of Jesus Christ, also includes strands of Parts 2 (Boundless Love) and 3 (To Bear Witness) because in her life and person the three movements are inextricably woven.

Welcoming Jesus, Our Life

What has come into being in him was life, and the life was the light of all people.

John 1:3–4

He, being God, became man,
in all things like us, except in sin,
and He proclaimed very clearly
that he had come to give the
good news.

Mother Teresa

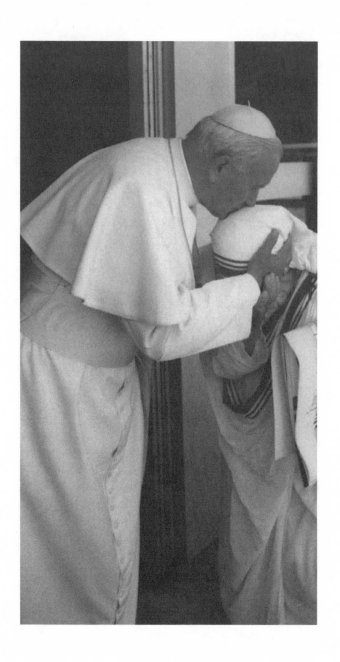

Mother Teresa found the Incarnation both a fathomless mystery and a gift beyond our gratitude. The coming of Jesus, true God and true man, gave her great joy. The Word made Flesh revealed clearly the nobility of human nature, a truth to be welcomed, celebrated, and passed on in loving service:

> Let us pray that we shall be able
> to welcome Jesus at Christmas,
> not in the cold manger of a
> selfish heart, but in a heart full
> of love, compassion, joy and
> peace, a heart warm with love
> for one another.

In Mary Mother Teresa saw a true missionary who courageously accepted being the handmaid of the Lord, although she knew not where that yes would take her. The newly pregnant Mary did not hesitate to make the difficult journey to see Elizabeth and share her good news. Nor did she shrink from serving Elizabeth, who was heavy with child. In her womb, Elizabeth's son John leapt for joy at the presence of the yet-to-be-born Messiah. Mother Teresa connects Mary's life with ours:

> Our Lady received Him
> in her womb with a humble
> heart, with a pure heart,

> then she went in haste to give
> Jesus to others.
> She went into the house of
> Elizabeth just to be the
> handmaid.
> … Mary taught us to serve,
> to love one another.

Those who seek Mother Teresa's guidance should look to that simple peasant home in Nazareth for the roots of her humility. She absorbed the example of Mary ("Let it be with me according to your word" [Lk 1:38b]). And she modeled herself after the Son who came into the world a poor, helpless infant and had to escape persecution by fleeing into Egypt. Reflecting on these things, Mother Teresa observed:

> At Christmas, we see Jesus as a
> little babe — helpless and poor.
> And He came to love and to be
> loved. How can we love Jesus in
> the world today?
> By loving Him in my husband,
> my wife, my children,
> my brothers and sisters, my
> parents, my neighbors, the poor.

Mother Teresa's daily life of prayer, adoration, and Eucharist enriched her understanding of scripture passages that many may take for granted. The nativity narratives are as familiar as our own family stories. However, if we take the time to reflect on

18

them, we might arrive at insights similar to those of Mother Teresa:

> In heaven everything was beautiful yet, what attracted Him?
> The Son of God wanted to feel what it means to be a human being; to be locked up for nine months, so dependent on a mother. That is why we say, "He, being rich, became poor" — so helpless!

Mother Teresa understood completely the reality of Jesus' thirty years of ordinary family life. She saw that, other than his appearance with the elders in the temple at the age of twelve, he had remained completely anonymous. Perhaps he even appeared to be "just wasting time." Yet, like every person, Jesus was passing through the stages of maturity that would prepare him for his mission.

Like the tree growing from the seed, he grew in wisdom quietly and gradually. His fellow townsfolk saw nothing more than a village carpenter until the day when he first began to teach them in the synagogue. Mother Teresa noted how Jesus' early years continue today.

> That silence, which Jesus kept for 30 years at Nazareth ...
> He keeps it even now in the tabernacle, always making intercession for us.

Mother Teresa often recommended "going back to Nazareth" to reflect on the meaning of the Incarnation and the magnitude of the Father's love. And we need not wait until Advent to focus on the greatest gift we have received — as well as the greatest gift we can give. She reminds us:

> Let us not forget the best and the most wonderful Gift that God has given to us — Jesus.
> And let us give Jesus to each other, beginning in our families.

Befriending Jesus, Our Companion

I have called you friends, because I have made known to you everything that I have heard from my Father.

John 15:15

Jesus is my Life.
Jesus is my only Love.
Jesus is my All in All.
Jesus is my Everything.

Mother Teresa

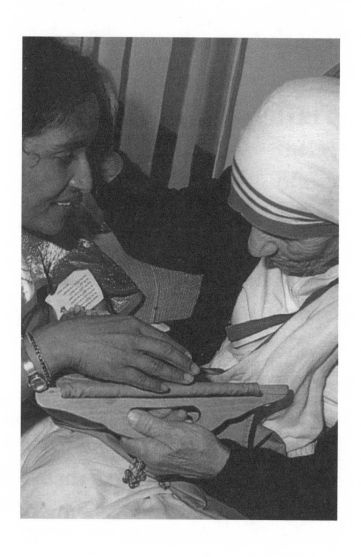

Mother Teresa would be the first to say that without the friendship with Jesus that sustained her, she could never have persevered in her daily life of service. When she says, "Jesus is my Everything," we know that she speaks the truth. And we suspect that the closer our own companionship with Jesus becomes, the more rewarding and fruitful our lives will be.

We might ask Mother Teresa, "Who is Jesus for you?" She is well prepared to respond because she has reflected deeply on the gospel story in which Jesus asked the disciples, "But who do you say that I am?" (Mt 16:15). Peter's response overjoyed his Teacher. "You are the Messiah, the Son of the living God" (16:16). The Holy Spirit invites us too to hear Jesus' question as a personal invitation.

In her meditation on this crucial question of Jesus, Mother Teresa begins her response with basic statements of belief, such as "You are God," "You are the Second Person of the Blessed Trinity," "You are the beloved Son." She goes on to name Jesus "Word made Flesh" and "Bread of Life." Writing more and more personally, she names Jesus:

> The Word — to be spoken,
> the Truth — to be told,
> the Way — to be walked,
> the Light — to be lit,
> the Life — to be lived,
> the Love — to be loved.

These words invite us to consider how we proclaim Jesus by the way we live, seek guidance from him as our way, center our days on him out of love. Mother Teresa continues, identifying Jesus as:

> the Hungry — to be fed,
> the Thirsty — to be satiated,
> the Naked — to be clothed,
> the Homeless — to be taken in,
> the Sick — to be healed.

As we might expect from a saint, the identities of Jesus become more difficult to recognize. Often, as we shoulder our demanding jobs and juggle our financial worries, the faces of the jobless and penniless do not register on our mental screens. And when the sick are outside our family circles, we may not remember to seek them out in their nursing homes and hospitals. Once again Mother Teresa urges us on with the following descriptions of a Jesus who we may not usually accept into our company:

> the Lonely — to be loved,
> the Unwanted — to be wanted,
> the Leper — to wash his wounds,
> the Beggar — to give him a smile,
> the Drunkard — to listen to him,
> the Retarded — to protect him,
> the Little One — to embrace him,
> the Blind — to lead him,
> the Dumb — to speak for him.
> the Crippled — to walk with him,

the Drug Addict — to befriend him,
the Prostitute — to remove from
danger and befriend,
the Prisoner — to be visited,
the Old — to be served.

Saints have a way of stretching us and taking us places we would rather not go. Tending to the needs of drunkards, outcasts, prostitutes, and prisoners may not come easily to those who have never seen in such faces the face of Christ. Making the time and practicing the patience to walk with the blind, the crippled, the senile, and the addicted requires a large-hearted commitment from any Christian. Yet as their love matures, those who befriend Jesus will seek to be his companion in all of his guises.

"You did it to me," I call this the
Gospel in five fingers ... And
St. John tells us that "if anyone
says, I love God, yet hates his
brother, he is a liar. One who has
no love for the brother whom he
has seen cannot love the God
whom he has not seen."
Look at your fingers often and
remind yourself of this love.

We might add: In whose face have I seen Jesus today? Did I look for him in any faces that I have previously ignored? How have I befriended them? Where might I seek Jesus tomorrow? As Mother

Teresa pointed out, a companion of Jesus thrives on prayer and meditation, the Eucharist and adoration. Just as human relationships require attentive nurturing, so we must not consign our friendship with Jesus to Sundays only. We must keep the inner flame of love steadily burning. Mother Teresa reminds us:

> **A Christian is a tabernacle of the living God.**

Praying with Jesus, Our Bread

I am the living bread that came down from heaven. Whoever eats of this bread will live forever; and the bread that I will give for the life of the world is my flesh.... Those who eat my flesh and drink my blood abide in me, and I in them.

John 6:51, 56

Jesus in the Eucharist necessarily leads us to Jesus in the poor. We need to be pure of heart to see Jesus in the person of the poor, for a pure heart can see God.

Mother Teresa

Whatever the demands on her time, energy, and compassion, Mother Teresa began every day with Mass and communion. She could not imagine being deprived of the Bread of Life for a single day. She often observed that the lives of the Missionaries of Charity were "woven with the Eucharist." To not participate in the Lord's Supper when it was readily available would be as foreign to Teresa as dressing in haute couture. She considered a day without the Eucharist empty and useless. She saw the unmistakable connection between the works of mercy and the Body and Blood of Christ.

> The Eucharist and the Poor we
> must never separate.
> … If we really believe that He,
> Jesus is in the appearance of
> bread and He, Jesus is in the
> hungry, the naked, the sick, the
> lonely, unloved, the homeless,
> the hopeless then our lives will
> be more and more woven with
> this deep faith in Jesus, the
> Bread of Life.

In the emaciated face of a dying street person Mother Teresa saw the same Jesus she had received that morning in communion. She saw no difference between the love that drove Jesus to become the bread of life, and the love that consequently drove her to give bread to the hungry. She observed:

> **Christ made Himself Bread of Life to satisfy our hunger for His love, and He makes Himself the Hungry One so that we may satisfy His hunger for our love.**

During her daily prayer, the founder of the Missionaries of Charity included a period of adoration before the Blessed Sacrament. No matter how tired she was, these times of silent prayer restored her. To her, an active life not fueled by faithful prayer was "suicide for our faith and love." As she said:

> **Love to pray — feel often during the day the need for prayer and take trouble to pray.**

Perhaps because she herself spent so many hours in wordless prayer even as she was passionately drawn to the active life, Mother Teresa often reiterated the need for regular periods of silence: "We cannot put ourselves directly in the presence of God if we do not practice internal and external silence." For her, that meant observing the silence of Mary who, when confronted with the mystery of her son's mission, "treasured all these things in her heart" (Lk 2:51). Teresa taught that anyone who aspired to be a prayerful person must become a soul of deep silence.

> We too ... must learn that
> "silence" which will enable us
> to ponder His Words in our
> hearts and so grow in love.
> We cannot love nor serve —
> unless we learn to ponder in
> our hearts.

Like so many saints before her, Mother Teresa comprehended the voice of the psalmist: "Be still, and know that I am God!" (46:10). In a world engulfed by the relentless sounds of radio, TV, CDs, DVDs, video games, and cell phones, she knew our need for a brief daily retreat into silence. She mirrored her Teacher who, in the midst of his demanding ministry, went up on the mountain by himself to pray. Her words are a gentle invitation:

> Silence of the eyes ... will always
> help us to see God.
> Our eyes are so like two windows
> through which Christ or the world
> comes into our hearts.
> Often we need great courage to
> keep them closed.

Along with contemplative silence, Mother Teresa likewise recommended the practice of spiritual reading. She would certainly agree that many books, from the lives of the saints to the reflections of contemporary spiritual directors, can inspire. However, we should not be surprised that she focuses on one book before all others.

> The New Testament will help you
> to know Christ better, love him
> more tenderly and serve Him with
> great zeal.

Describing further the integral value of reflecting on scripture as a part of daily prayer, Mother Teresa encourages us:

> Jesus, God made man,
> has come to reveal the Father's
> love to us. Listen in prayer and
> deep faith to His teachings and
> make a strong resolution to do
> what He says.

Mother Teresa's prayer life was a source of energy, vision, direction, and joy. She would not compromise it for other concerns that seemed more pressing. She once put the matter succinctly:

> The fruit of silence is prayer
> The fruit of prayer is faith
> The fruit of faith is love
> The fruit of love is service
> The fruit of service is peace.

Again, she links prayer and providing for Christ's least ones. The Eucharist, silence, adoration, scripture reflection draw us ever closer to the loving Father Jesus taught us to approach confidently in the Lord's Prayer. Like the wise mother she was, Teresa put it plainly:

In the silence of your heart, God speaks, and we listen, and then, from the fullness of our hearts, we speak. And that listening and that speaking is prayer.

Responding to Jesus, Our Call

Who saved us and called us with a holy calling, not according to our works but according to his own purpose and grace. This grace was given to us in Christ Jesus before the ages began.

2 Timothy 1:9

We are called to be holy — all of us — it is a simple duty for you and for me.

Mother Teresa

During her lifetime, everyone around the world recognized the holiness of Mother Teresa. Christians, Hindus, Muslims, Jews, and even those who professed no faith at all concurred. They knew her by the fruits of her labors. And they knew that she labored not just for her fellow Christians but for every poor and dying person. Like Jesus himself, she did not limit who received her compassionate service.

Mother Teresa would be among the first to point out that the terms holiness and vocation apply to everyone — not just to those in the vowed religious life or the priesthood. She observed:

> We have to become holy in whatever life God has put us … whatever He picks — as a mother, as a father, as a priest, as a sister, whatever it is, a young man, a young woman — whatever we are, wherever we are, we have to bring holiness there. And holiness is nothing but acceptance of the will of God with a big smile.

This description leaves no doubt that every person, married or single, young or old, can, with God's grace, respond to Jesus' call to holiness. Our particular circumstances matter not at all. The only garden in which sanctity will not grow is the untended one. Mother Teresa often pointed out that a

simple smile or a listening ear draws people closer
to God and helps the provider grow in holiness.
Like Thérèse of Lisieux, she believed in doing
small things with great love. And she prayed that all
Christians might fully experience and share the joy
Jesus intended for them.

> The joy of the presence of Jesus,
> you must be able to give wherever
> you go. But you cannot give what
> you don't have. That's why you
> need a pure heart, a pure heart
> that you will receive as a fruit
> of your prayer, as a fruit of your
> oneness with Christ.

In these words Mother Teresa assures that joy,
one of the gifts of the Holy Spirit, is a sign of holiness and of God's presence. If we recall the faces
of those who have attracted us to God, we know
that Mother Teresa is right. She reminds us:

> May you keep the joy of loving
> Jesus in your hearts and share
> that joy with all you come in
> contact with. That radiating
> joy is something real, for you
> have no reason not to be happy
> because you have Christ with
> you — Christ in your hearts,
> Christ in the Eucharist,
> Christ in the poor that you meet,

Christ in the smile that you give
and in the smile that you receive.

We cannot but admire the simplicity of Mother Teresa's advice and see its practical applications in our everyday lives. To smile at an exhausted fellow commuter on the subway or listen to a disgruntled passenger at the airport, to give up your place in the supermarket line gladly to the mother of a whining child, or to yield courteously to an angry driver in a traffic jam is to share a little taste of holiness.

Of our common call to sanctity, Mother Teresa observed:

Where does sanctity begin? In
your own hearts; that's why we
need that continual prayer —
to keep our hearts clean,
for the clean heart becomes
the tabernacle of the living God.

She reminds us that the call to holiness may also require more far-reaching sacrifices as our circumstances demand: leaving home or home-land, enduring intolerance or even persecution on account of one's faith, being misunderstood and unjustly punished, devoting years rather than days to serving the people of God. Of vocations to the religious life or the priesthood in the church today, Mother Teresa said:

I think it's beginning again to
come with greater strength …
we must not lose confidence …

> All these years of not having
> vocations is gone, but today we
> may get some good vocations so
> let us be busy with them today.

Those who came from wealthy families to join the Missionaries of Charity edified her. When she asked them why they did so, their responses always contained two significant words: Jesus and poverty. These candidates for religious life welcomed the prospect of depending not on a hefty bank account or a privileged rank in society, but on divine providence itself. Mother Teresa shared with them the story of her "second calling" by which the Holy Spirit summoned her from a teaching order to the streets of Calcutta. Although she did not know exactly how she was to serve, she was certain that she was called to the poorest of the poor. She later recalled:

> The message was quite clear.
> I was to leave the convent and
> work with the poor while living
> among them. It was an order.
> I knew where I belonged, but I
> did not know how to get there.

Like many, Mother Teresa had lived well with all the material comforts of middle- and upper-class daily life. But once she had accepted her second call, she never turned back to that life of greater ease. Whether involved in direct ministry to the poor or not, we can reflect on Jesus' call to live more simply, to rely less on tangible things,

40

and to share more of what we have with those who do not have enough. He does not impose this. But he invites us to remain open to any as-yet-unidentified call from the harvest master. As Mother Teresa pointed out:

> If Jesus comes in your life, and
> wants you then to follow Him,
> as a priest or as a religious, have
> the courage to say: "Yes" for He
> loves you tenderly. He is offering
> you His lifelong, faithful, personal
> friendship....

Being Faithful to Jesus' Poor Ones

Blessed are you who are poor, for yours is the kingdom of God.

Luke 6:20

The poor are the gift of God for us. They are great people. They are very lovable people.

Mother Teresa

When a priest-friend asked about her method of working with the poor, Mother Teresa explained that the Missionaries of Charity did not wait for the needy to be brought to them. Although the police or the neighbors sometimes delivered the poor to their doorstep, most were found by searching diligently for them. And when the missionaries found the destitute ones, they welcomed them as invited guests. Each poor, sick, or dying person became one of "Mother Teresa's people." She and her sisters never turned anyone down or judged someone as unworthy of their attention. They could not conceive of preaching Christ's universal love while practicing any form of intolerance.

> I see human beings as God's children with the right to live in love, peace and harmony. I call on each and every one to live in love and to share the joy of loving by helping each other to grow in holiness, serving one another and caring for each other's needs.

Mother Teresa truly saw the poor as God's gift to those who have all they need and places to live. She was sure that Jesus would judge us on how much love we had invested in our responses to the hungry, the sick, those whom society considers without value. To her way of thinking, the poor have much to offer.

Our poor people throughout
the world are very wonderful
people.… The trust and the
gratitude and the love they give;
as some people who had come
to help us … said that they had
received much more than they
had given to the people whom
they served and this is exactly
what each one of us feels when
we are in contact with the poorest
of the poor — the enrichment we
receive from them.

Emphasizing how Jesus chose to be born in poverty, Mother Teresa felt that the wealthy who cling to their riches are, in truth, "very poor." When they choose to put their substance at the service of others, however, they achieve true wealth that lasts forever. She would advise them, with Saint Paul, "to be rich in good works, generous, and ready to share" in order to amass a lasting treasure (1 Tm 6:18). The Missionaries of Charity live out their call to help the poor, whether in body or in soul. Nevertheless, Mother Teresa loved tremendously those who had the least of this world's goods. She said:

We must thank the poor for
allowing us to love Jesus in them
because Jesus said "Whatever
you do to the least of my brethren
you do it to me."

Those with only a passing acquaintance with Mother Teresa realize her passionate defense of the unborn child. For her, the poor and least included the child in the womb, completely at the mercy of others.

> The child is the most beautiful gift
> of God to a family, to a nation.
> Let us never refuse this gift of
> God. My prayer for each one of
> you is that you may always have
> the faith to see and love God in
> each person including the unborn.

Mother Teresa saw abortion as the greatest danger to world peace because it showed a complete disregard for human life. She consistently underscored the truth that no human hand should ever be raised to kill life. She insisted that no person had the right to destroy the unborn child.

> The greatest destroyer of peace
> in the world today is abortion.
> If a mother can kill her own child,
> what is there to stop you and me
> from killing each other? The only
> one who has the right to take life
> is the One who has created it.

She had the highest respect for parents who welcomed new babies into their families despite the hardships they might face. She praised those parents eager to adopt unwanted infants. And she encouraged all parents to be faithful to the Teacher who counseled: "Let the little children come to me" (Mk 10:14).

Also close to her heart were the sick and the dying. She prayed that more Christians would take personally Jesus' promise: "For I ... was sick and you took care of me" (Mt 25:36). By washing, tending, and holding the sick Mother Teresa expressed love in action.

> In Kalighat ... the Sisters and volunteers serve the poorest of the poor with so much tender love and compassion without being concerned as to religion, nationality, caste or color. The sick may be Hindu, Muslim or Christian — all receive the care and love they need.

In Calcutta Mother Teresa and the missionaries tended the lepers; in Brooklyn they cared for those dying of AIDS. She observed that unless the Sisters and Brothers saw Jesus in the emaciated and deformed faces before them, they would find ministering to these patients extremely difficult. Medicines and treatments alone could never heal those from whom society retreats in fear or judgment.

> There are many poor people that need love and compassion; that need your hands to serve them; that need your hearts to love them.... People are not hungry just for bread, they are hungry

for love. People are not naked
only for a piece of cloth; they are
naked for that human dignity.
People are not only homeless for
a room made of bricks; but they
are homeless — being rejected,
unwanted, unloved. Jesus says:
"Love as I have loved you: I have
wanted you. I have loved you and
you love, as I have loved you."

Once again Mother Teresa returns to the ne-
cessity of living in love day by given day. Without a
firm commitment to love, we cannot persevere in
either the spiritual works of mercy, like forgiveness,
or the corporal works of mercy, like providing for
the homeless. Her inspired words identifying the
poorest of the poor, challenge us to a clearer vision
of those awaiting our compassionate care.

There is so much suffering
everywhere. Suffering from
hunger, from homelessness,
from all kinds of diseases.
But I still think that the greatest
suffering is being lonely, being
unwanted, being unloved, just
having no one, having forgotten
what it is like to have the human
touch, human love, what it is to
be wanted, what it is to be loved,
what it is to have your own people.

Part 2

Boundless Love

In 1948, riding a train to Darjeeling, Sister Teresa received the invitation she could not refuse. This "call within a call" was the sure conviction that she was to follow Christ into the streets and slums to care for the poorest of the poor. Although she responded with an unqualified "Yes!", Mother Teresa later said that leaving the Sisters of Loreto was the greatest sacrifice of her life. She loved her community and had received an admirable religious formation in their midst.

Barriers of every kind fell before her as Sr. Teresa set her indomitable will to do what Jesus required of her. She took an intensive nursing course to prepare herself to provide basic medical care. In Calcutta, she moved to the upper floor of Michael Gomes' house and began by teaching orphans and poor children in the streets. Through the children, she moved on to their families. Within two years, she had founded the Missionaries of Charity, a congregation that immediately attracted several of her former pupils.

Taking her cue from the poor themselves, Mother Teresa began providing services that became the hallmark of the Missionaries of Charity: feeding the starving, rescuing those dying on the streets, caring for orphans, sheltering the homeless, nursing the lepers, and offering hospitality to those shunned by others. At a time when religious vocations were waning, the Missionaries of Charity never lacked for new candidates who were irresistibly drawn to serving Jesus "in his distressing disguise."

The woman who set this global movement in motion was driven by a love that can only be described in biblical terms: "For love is strong as death, passion fierce as the grave. Its flashes are flashes of fire, a raging flame" (Sg 8:6).

Loving Others as Jesus Loves Us

I give you a new commandment, that you love one another. Just as I have loved you, you also should love one another.

John 13:34

Don't be afraid to love as Jesus loves you.

Mother Teresa

Some Christians shrink from the seeming impossibility of loving as Jesus loved, but Mother Teresa took the Son of God at his word. She knew that he would not ask us to do anything beyond our capabilities. She knew Jesus had promised that "for God all things are possible" (Mk 10:27). These words assured her that any person, no matter how physically or spiritually destitute, appears loveable to one who loves with the heart of Christ.

> I feel more and more that the
> poor are the hope of salvation
> of mankind, because we are
> going to be judged at the hour
> of death with what we have been
> to them, what we have done for
> them. Jesus Christ said that on
> the judgment day, He is going
> to judge us with these words —
> "I was hungry and you fed me,
> I was naked and you clothed
> me, I was homeless and you
> took me in."

To mirror in our own lives the love Jesus has given, is giving, and will give does not deprive us of any happiness rightfully ours. Mother Teresa's heroic service to the least did not leave her feeling deprived or depressed. On the contrary, the bountiful flow of love she poured out on others returned to her in an even greater portion. Others could see in her the fulfillment of Jesus' assurance: "The measure you give will be the measure you get, and still more will be given you" (Mk 4:24). As she testified:

> Go in haste to give the joy
> of loving, the joy of sharing,
> for you have received not
> to keep but to share.

If we have not yet experienced it for ourselves, hands-on caring for the destitute and the dying may seem an unlikely source of happiness. However, Mother Teresa never ceased speaking of the strength, the comfort, and the joy she felt in her ministry. She never lost sight of the Jesus who walked with her among the needy ones. And it was he who received her loving service. For this truth, she was profoundly grateful.

> Our works are only expressions
> of our love for Christ.
> Our hearts need to be full of
> love for him and since we have
> to express that love in action,
> naturally then the poorest of
> the poor are the means of
> expressing our love for God.

The failure of so many to recognize Jesus in the world today made Mother Teresa grieve. Rushing through their daily rounds, they do not stop to seek him in prayer or in silence, in their neighbor or in the homeless person sleeping on a park bench. They allow exterior noise and interior chatter to muffle the still, small voice of God. Only the spiritually aware see Jesus whenever he approaches. Mother Teresa observed:

> It is Jesus who feels in Himself the hunger of the poor, their thirst and their tears.... Jesus became so much one with the poor that He took the form of a servant.
> Our faith in Jesus must lead us to love, and love must lead to service. But service is not possible without prayer.

Knowing human nature as well as she did, Mother Teresa realized how the selfishness and materialism so common in our culture can stunt our faith. Faith and love, she believed, "walk side by side." Thus, a faith that does not do the works of love is inauthentic. Saint James put it even more explicitly: "For just as the body without the spirit is dead, so faith without works is also dead" (2:26). Lest we miss the opportunities placed directly in our paths, Mother Teresa pointed out:

> Maybe in our own family we have somebody who is feeling lonely, who is feeling sick, who is feeling worried. Are we there? Are we willing to give until it hurts in order to be with our

families, or do we put our own interests first?

Mother Teresa often counseled well-meaning Christians who sought the freedom of going off to the missions to look for the unloved first in their family or neighborhood. She never limited the responsibility to love to the family. But she did say that it began there. What we practice in the family circle must ripple into larger and larger circles of universal love. As she said:

> My brother, my sister is that
> hungry one, that naked one,
> that homeless one, that lonely
> one, that unwanted one —
> they are my brothers and my
> sisters because Christ Himself
> has told us so.

Being Reconciled Through Jesus

We entreat you on behalf of Christ,
be reconciled to God.

2 Corinthians 5:20

Reconciliation begins not first
with others but with ourselves:
by allowing Jesus to clean us —
to forgive us, to love us.

Mother Teresa

Whether we refer to the sacrament as penance, reconciliation, or confession, Mother Teresa placed this experience of God's pardon high on her list of necessities for those who follow Jesus. To simply abide by the Church's requirement of an annual confession would be, to her mind, a sure way of depriving oneself of a grace-filled experience. It would also be a way of depriving Jesus of the opportunity, through the ministry of the confessor, of saying aloud clearly to each person, "Your sins are forgiven." Yet she knew that many Catholics, held back by pride or fear, resentment or misunderstanding, deny themselves the benefits of the sacrament. She observed:

> One thing is necessary for
> us — confession.
> Confession is nothing
> but humility in action.
> We call it Penance but really
> it is a sacrament of love,
> a sacrament of forgiveness....
> It is a place where I allow Jesus
> to take away from me everything
> that divides, that destroys.
> Be very simple and
> child-like in confession.

When Mother Teresa recommends confession as an act of humility, a familiar image underscores her counsel: the bent body, the weathered face, the simple white and blue sari, the sturdy sandals. If such a renowned religious figure could appear so self-effacing before the entire world, could anyone doubt her even greater humility before God in the confessional? She personified the little ones of whom Jesus said: "Unless you change and become like children, you will never enter the kingdom of heaven. Whoever becomes humble like this child is the greatest in the kingdom of heaven" (Mt 18:3–4). Recognizing her as one of these little ones, we honor the authenticity of her advice:

> The beginning of holiness is a good confession. We are all sinners.... I am a sinner with sin. When I make a good confession I become a sinner without sin.

Because the words of the Lord's Prayer are so familiar, we readily forget that Jesus attached a condition to only one petition: "Forgive us our sins as we forgive those who sin against us." Mother Teresa often stressed how crucial it was that we learn to pardon if we hoped to be pardoned by our Father in heaven. As a spiritual work of mercy, forgiveness strengthens us whenever we practice it. She counseled:

We cannot forgive unless we
know that we need forgiveness,
and forgiveness is the beginning
of love.

We are mistaken, Mother Teresa pointed out, to think of confession or reconciliation as a private matter between the individual and God. All sin has social ramifications, weakening the bonds between people and, at times, abusing God's marvelous creation. To celebrate the sacrament of penance is to perform an act of love for God, for humanity and for the world around us.

Recognizing that a burden of guilt convinces many that they do not deserve God's forgiveness, Mother Teresa had these encouraging words:

It is so wonderful to think that
you and I — it doesn't matter
how full of misery or greatness
we are — are precious to Him
because He loves us.

A spiritual mentor and mother to millions throughout the world, Mother Teresa reached out to those who felt compelled to hide from God. She understood that those who avoid confession include sinners who have already suffered greatly from the consequences of their own and others' misdeeds. She assured them:

He loves you always,
even when you don't feel worthy.
If not accepted by others,
even by yourself sometimes —
He is the one who always
accepts you.... Only believe —
you are precious to Him.
Bring all you are suffering to His
feet — only open your heart to be
loved by Him as you are.
He will do the rest.

As did Teresa of Avila, Mother Teresa understood that spiritual maturity requires self-knowledge. A discerning confessor or spiritual director can help us to recognize the precious things already in our souls as well as those things that need to be converted. Saint Teresa called self-knowledge "the bread that must be eaten with every dish." Mother Teresa would heartily agree.

If we face God in prayer and
silence God speaks to us.
Then, only, we know that we
are nothing. It is only when we
realize our nothingness, our
emptiness, that God can fill us
with Himself.

Once more we hear the voice of the diminutive saint who recognized daily her absolute dependence on Jesus. No matter how much she accomplished or how much praise she received, Mother Teresa never dismissed her need for daily prayer, Eucharist, and frequent confession. She knew the source of her strength: "Be strong in the Lord and in the strength of his power" (Eph 6:10).

Accepting the Cross with Jesus

Whoever does not carry the cross and
follow me cannot be my disciple.

Luke 14:27

We all have to take the cross,
we all have to follow Christ
to Calvary, if we want to rise
with Him.

Mother Teresa

No Christian who served suffering humanity as faithfully as Mother Teresa could fail to be devoted to the way of the cross. Whether in praying the traditional devotion of the fourteen stations or in meditating on the passion of Christ in the gospels, she consistently connected Jesus' suffering and our own. She saw what suffering and unending pain mean for those who unite themselves with Christ. As Peter advised the early Christians: "But rejoice insofar as you are sharing Christ's sufferings, so that you may also be glad and shout for joy when his glory is revealed" (1 Pt 4:13).

Mother Teresa reflected on the first, second, and third stations in this way:

> In our Stations of the Cross
> we see Jesus, as the poor and
> hungry, falling. Are we there to
> help Him? Are we there with our
> sacrifice, with our bread, real
> bread.... There are thousands
> and thousands of people who die
> for a little bit of love, for a little bit
> of recognition.

Mother Teresa did not pray "the way" as a pious practice removed from everyday life. In the stations, she could identify with Jesus and with those he encountered on the way to Calvary. She asked herself if she had responded to the hungry and thirsty, the poor and the exhausted, the burdened and the fallen as though they were Jesus himself. When we pity his sufferings without relieving those of our neighbor, we are like people who, though our hearts are from him, honor God with our lips alone (see Is 29:13).

Reflecting on stations four through ten, Mother Teresa observes:

> And we have that fourth Station
> of the Cross where He meets
> His mother. Are we a mother
> to the suffering?... Simon of
> Cyrene took up the cross and
> followed Jesus, helped Jesus to
> carry His cross.... And Veronica.
> Are we Veronica to our poor? ...
> Again Jesus falls.
> How many times we have picked
> up people from the street who
> have lived like animals and long
> to die like angels. Are we there
> to lift them up?... That is Jesus
> who needs your hand to wipe
> [His] face. Are you there to do it
> or do you pass by?

Mother Teresa asks us to consider how we are mother or father to those who, like Mary's son, suffer persecution and are unjustly punished. Are we, like Mary herself, present to those bowed down by crosses imposed upon them?

Mother Teresa then turns our attention to Simon and Veronica, guiding us to reflect on how we might help others shoulder the crosses of chronic illness, physical or mental impairment, addiction or depression. How do we wipe the sweaty and furrowed brows of those who are destitute and have no one to aid them? When we encounter those fallen by the wayside of life, do we lift them up or pass them by? (See Lk 10:29–36 to review Jesus' parable of the Good Samaritan.)

In the final four stations, Mother Teresa invites us to consider that just as his enemies treated Jesus no better than an animal, so our society considers some as having little or no value. In their poverty, they are humiliated or simply disregarded. Mother Teresa reflects:

> [Jesus] was stripped of His
> clothes. Today the little one
> before its birth is stripped of love.
> It must die because we don't
> want that child....
> Jesus [is] crucified.
> How many handicapped people,
> mentally retarded, young people
> fill the hospitals? How many there
> are in our own homes?...
> Everywhere there are hungry
> people looking up at you....
> Do not turn your back on the
> poor, for they are Christ.

Mother Teresa always saw the suffering Christ reflected in the unwanted unborn child. And she fixed her gaze upon the impaired ones whom society often hides away, leaving them to walk their way of the cross alone. She had a special place in her heart for the parents of an extensively disabled and disfigured child who called their child the "Professor of Love" because that is what he taught them. Likewise, Mother Teresa felt compassion for those who made the mistake of believing that their suffering proved that God had abandoned them. She assured them:

> Suffering is a gift of God.
> It's a sign that we have come so
> close to Him that we can share
> His passion, that we can share
> the joy of loving with Him in pain,
> in suffering. Suffering is not a
> punishment, it is a gift.
> A gift that purifies us and
> sanctifies us.
> It is really the kiss of Jesus.

Those who seek to hasten God's reign of justice and peace must be willing to carry the cross as Jesus willingly did. When we feel that our suffering is in vain, Mother Teresa directs our gaze to Calvary. She observes:

> Jesus ... gave up everything to
> do God's will, to show us that
> we too must be willing to give

72

up everything to do God's will
to love one another as He loves
each one of us.

Knowing that artistic depictions of Jesus' suffering, such as Michelangelo's *Pietà,* or Mel Gibson's
The Passion of the Christ, fills us with compassion,
Mother Teresa urged all Christians toward the
much harder task of seeing him just as clearly in
the poor, the sick, the dying, the unloved. Despite
the cost, we must be willing to enter into the suffering of others. At times the sheer weight of the
world's suffering and of our own limitations can
overwhelm us. Mother Teresa advises, however:

Suffering in itself is nothing;
but suffering shared with Christ's
Passion is a wonderful gift.
Let us ... gladly make many
sacrifices and offer up our
sufferings. Just as Jesus'
suffering and death led to
the joy of Easter, so we will
share in the joy and glory of the
Risen Christ inasmuch as we
share in His passion.

Claiming the Joy of Jesus Risen

I have said these things to you so that
my joy may be in you, and that your
joy may be complete.

John 15:11

Remember that the Passion of
Christ ends always in the joy of the
Resurrection of Christ, so when
you feel in your own heart the
suffering of Christ, remember the
Resurrection has to come, the joy
of Easter has to dawn.

Mother Teresa

Mother Teresa considered Good Friday one of the most important days of the liturgical year. Her life's work resonated deeply with Jesus' suffering in his passion and crucifixion. Good Friday, however, provided the prelude to Mother Teresa's most beloved feast, the one promising eternal happiness for all who have been faithful to Christ. We can picture her face wreathed in smiles as she said:

> Easter is one of those beautiful
> days when we rejoice.
> And we must always remember
> never to allow anything like
> sorrow or pain so to fill us as to
> forget that Christ has risen for
> you and for me.

Living among the poorest of the poor, cradling the diminished bodies of the dying, and rescuing the dispossessed from the streets might well have caused the cross to predominate in Mother Teresa's ministry. Yet that did not happen. Like the disciples rushing eagerly back to Jerusalem from Emmaus, she owned the joy of the risen Lord. And she shared that joy with all who were overcome by sorrow, all who had forgotten that Good Friday was not the end of the story. Not for Jesus. Not for us. She put it very simply:

> We must be able to radiate joy,
> to radiate the joy of Christ;
> because that is a sign that
> He is with us; because
> His presence should always,
> always produce this joy. And so,
> let the people look up and see
> only Jesus in you and in me.

Christians with gloomy faces who have "given up on the world" make poor ambassadors for Christ. Their pessimism drives others away from him and from the church. On the other hand, listen to the inviting voice of Mother Teresa who attracted countless seekers and unbelievers to the faith she espoused:

> Without joy there is no love and
> love without joy is not true love.
> And so we need to bring that love
> and that joy into the world
> of today.

Just as every Sunday the church celebrates "a little Easter," Mother Teresa would advocate our daily recollection of Christ's glorious resurrection. She urged those who could to participate in the Eucharist daily. Others who could not participate at Mass so frequently might make it their practice to spend a few minutes each day savoring a gospel verse such as: "They said to each other, 'Were not our hearts burning within us while he was talking to us on the road, while he was opening the scriptures to us?'" (Lk 24:32). To do so is to make an investment in replenishing our joy. This store of joy then illumines our lives and has its effect on those around us. Mother Teresa had a delightful image for it:

> Joy is a net of love by which we catch souls. Because we are full of joy everyone ... wants to be in our company to receive the light of Christ we possess.

After the disciples had encountered the risen Lord and been filled with the Holy Spirit, they gave free rein to their post-resurrection faith. Their joy, their hope, and their conviction were so contagious that three thousand people were converted in one day (see Acts 2:37–41). Mother Teresa knew firsthand how effective even a single joyful Christian can be in drawing others to Christ:

> Once a man came to Kalighat and he just walked in and went right in the ward. I was there. After a little while he came back and said to me, "I came here with so much hate in my heart, hate for God and hate for man. I came here empty, faithless, embittered and I saw a Sister inside giving

> her wholehearted attention to
> that patient there and I realized
> that God still loves; now I go out
> a different man. I believe there is
> a God and He loves us still."

In all of her contacts with those who did not yet know Jesus, Mother Teresa tried to show forth the joy of the Lord. She wanted others to see not only the great victory of the resurrection, but the joy that pervaded the life of Jesus and those who followed him. She observed:

> Joy was the characteristic
> mark of the first Christians.
> During the persecutions,
> people used to watch those
> who had this joy radiating on
> their faces....
> St. Paul ... always urged the
> early Christians to rejoice
> in the Lord always.
> His whole life can be summed
> up in one sentence,
> "I belong to Christ."
> Nothing can separate me
> from the love of Christ,
> neither sufferings nor
> persecutions nor anything.

Here Mother Teresa fastens on a bedrock truth that lies at the heart of our Christian faith. Even in the midst of his agony on the cross, Jesus harbored, like a candle in a storm, the joy of doing God's will fully, generously, and with perfect love. As Paul observes, "For the sake of the joy that lay before him he endured the cross, despising its shame, and has taken his seat at the right of the throne of God" (Heb 12:2). Our suffering, when united with his, does not preclude an invincible joy that no one can take away. His victory over death is our victory: "For the trumpet will sound, the dead will be raised incorruptible, and we will all be changed" (1 Cor 15:52).

Jesus in the Eucharist

The cup of blessing that we bless,
is it not a sharing in the blood of
Christ? The bread that we break, is
it not a sharing in the body of Christ?
Because there is one bread, we who
are many are one body, for we all partake of the one bread.

1 Corinthians 10:16–17

Jesus has made Himself the
Bread of Life, to give us life,
to give us love, to give us joy,
to give us strength.

Mother Teresa

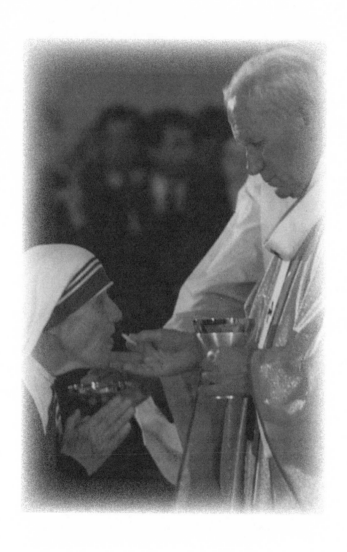

One of Mother Teresa's greatest joys was her community life, which began each day with the celebration of the Eucharist. Joined with her Missionaries of Charity, she experienced the kind of life Jesus' first followers shared. "They devoted themselves to the apostles' teaching and fellowship, to the breaking of bread and the prayers" (Acts 2:42). Recalling how the early Christians practiced their faith, Mother Teresa observed:

> We begin our day with prayer,
> Mass, Holy Communion and we
> end our day with Adoration of
> the Blessed Sacrament.
> Our lives are woven with the
> Eucharist and our love for Jesus,
> in action, is in the service of the
> poorest of the poor.

Always she connected her union with the Bread of Life with her service to those who had no bread. Her reception of Jesus in Holy Communion enabled her communion with those to whom he reached out most often in his earthly ministry. As she said:

> I believe the strength and the
> courage and the love and the
> work that we are doing for those
> thousands and thousands

> and thousands of people, it is
> not ours, it is … that our lives
> are very closely woven with the
> Eucharist.

Throughout her religious life Mother Teresa reflected on the meaning of the Eucharist as the church's greatest treasure and the source of our constancy in the faith. For her the real presence of Jesus in the consecrated bread and wine was far more than a doctrine to be believed. It was the reality by which she lived. To partake of such a treasure thoughtlessly or thanklessly was impossible for one who realized so deeply the Eucharist's inestimable value.

> Saint John Berchmans:
> of him it is said that he used
> to spend the first half of the day
> after Holy Communion in
> thanksgiving because Jesus
> had come into his heart and
> the second half in preparation
> because Jesus would come
> into his heart.

Joined to Christ and to each other through the celebration of the Mass, Mother Teresa and her Sisters went forth each day to share the Bread of Life with all who needed them. The founder would immediately correct anyone who suggested that it was she herself whom the poor sought with outstretched arms and pleading faces. She said:

The greatest hunger in the
world today is the hunger
for God. Jesus is the only one
who can answer that hunger.
Jesus has given Himself to us
in the Eucharist to satisfy our
hunger and He gives himself to
us in the poor so that we might
satisfy His hunger.

Mother Teresa would agree with these words of Cyril of Alexandria: "Just as if someone were to twist two pieces of wax together and melt them with a fire, so the two are made one, so too through participation in the Body of Christ and in His precious Blood, He is united to us and we to Him." To separate yourself from this sacrament of unity was like turning your back on a banquet in a time of hunger. For Mother Teresa, the Eucharist could never remain on the sidelines of her life. She noted:

We need that continual feeding;
that is why we begin the day at
half past four in the morning
and then we have Mass,
Holy Communion, meditation
and so on. Then, in the evening,
in all our houses we have the
hour of adoration.

To intensify their Eucharistic life, the Missionaries of Charity practice adoration of the Blessed

Sacrament. Although the forty hours of devotion and benediction waned after Vatican Council II, both are reappearing in parish life. Mother Teresa would support this revival wholeheartedly. She had experienced the benefits of meditating in the presence of the Blessed Sacrament. And she wanted others to do likewise.

> We find that through our daily
> Holy Hour our love for Jesus
> becomes more intimate,
> our love for each other more
> understanding, and our love for
> the poor more compassionate....
> Our Adoration has doubled the
> number of our vocations.

Many who visited Mother Teresa in Calcutta have testified to her deep devotion during these times of adoration. Most often visitors themselves would be invited — in a tone that did not take no for an answer — to join the Sisters before the Blessed Sacrament. Having removed their sandals or shoes at the chapel door and kneeling with Mother Teresa on woven mats before the monstrance, these visitors saw that she seemed to have emptied herself completely of all desires and needs save that for a total reliance on Jesus. She advised:

> May you discover that nowhere
> on earth are you more welcomed,
> nowhere on earth are you more

loved, than by Jesus, living and
truly present in the Most Blessed
Sacrament. The time you spend
with Jesus in the Blessed
Sacrament is the best time
that you will spend on earth.

Being joined to Jesus in a Eucharistic life was as necessary to Mother Teresa as breathing. She constantly shared this reality with others — especially those who came to consult or to join her in her work. When in 1989 her friend Fr. Lush Gjergji came from Albania to visit her in the hospital, Mother Teresa briefly greeted him. She then gave him advice that we might all consider in nurturing spiritual friendships and setting out on our own ministries:

First adore the Lord in the
tabernacle; then come
and we shall talk.

Part 3

To Bear Witness

The Western world learned of Mother Teresa through Malcolm Muggeridge. Fascinated by her self-sacrificing ministry to the poorest of the poor, this well-known British agnostic interviewed her in 1959 and was "transformed in her presence." Afterwards, he converted to Christianity. To share his admiration for the living saint who had shown him the light of Christ, in 1969 he made a television documentary, *Something Beautiful for God*. A book by the same title followed in 1971. Thus, the world beyond Calcutta came to learn that every person has been called to do "something beautiful for God."

As Mother Teresa and her work became more widely known, her Missionaries of Charity expanded and divided into branches of religious brothers and priests, contemplative Sisters and Brothers, Lay Missionaries of Charity, and the International Association of Co-Workers of Mother Teresa. This latter group includes those who help by offering prayer and practical support, raising funds, and gathering material resources. It also includes the Sick and Suffering Co-Workers who agree to "love and serve Jesus, not by what they offer, but by what they take." Here again Mother Teresa emphasizes how the poor and the sick give by receiving services from those who are materially or physically better off.

The Missionaries of Charity have now established more than 610 foundations in 123 countries. In 1997 her failing health convinced Mother Teresa to delegate leadership to Sr. Nirmala Joshi. Before her final illness, she made a final trip to Rome to see her dear friend Pope John Paul II, who saw in her "an icon of the Good Samaritan."

Undoubtedly the world at large agreed with him.

Bearing Witness to Jesus

Jesus said to them again, "Peace be with you. As the Father has sent me, so I send you."

John 20:21

The purpose of our missionary activity is: to bring the poor to Jesus and to bring Jesus to the poor.

Mother Teresa

Mother Teresa is known for her conviction that God had called her to bear witness to his presence among the poor in body, mind, or spirit. She took to heart the risen Lord's commissioning of her as a missionary. Thus, she left her homeland, her family, and her first religious vocation to fulfill her "call within a call." This second call required her and those who joined her to embrace the holy poverty that Jesus himself had lived. She emphasized how shameful it would be if the Missionaries of Charity were "wealthier than Jesus." Mother Teresa insisted:

> For me and my sisters poverty
> is freedom, and the less we
> have the more we can give.
> Poverty is love before it is
> renunciation. It is not that we
> cannot have luxuries.
> We choose not to have them.
> This freedom brings joy,
> and joy enables us to give
> in love until it hurts.

Mother Teresa never forgot that Jesus was born in a stable that belonged to someone else and that he was buried in a borrowed tomb. In his public ministry, he depended upon the support of others. When he sent out the Twelve to proclaim the kingdom of God, he told them: "Take nothing for your journey, no staff, nor bag, nor bread, nor money — not even an extra tunic" (Lk 9:3). Mother Teresa saw that:

> More than any other
> Congregation, we need
> poverty, real poverty.
> It gives us the detachment
> and the real freedom necessary
> to understand the very poor
> people with whom we work.

Their material simplicity and their willingness to enter into the lives of people who owned neither houses nor wardrobes, possessions nor securities of any kind has made Mother Teresa and her sister and brother missionaries appeal to everyone. Although few could imitate the Missionaries of Charity in their poverty, all their admirers could choose to "Live simply so that others might simply live." Of those who did choose to join her Mother Teresa said:

> The aim of the Missionaries of
> Charity is to quench the thirst
> of Jesus on the Cross for the
> love of souls by working for the
> salvation and sanctification of
> the poorest of the poor.
> A missionary must be
> a missionary of love ...

Mother Teresa understood well Jesus' parable of the Two Foundations. She knew that the person who listens to the words of Jesus but does not act on them is like a builder who fails to lay a foundation. When the rains come and the river overflows, that house is washed away. On the other hand, one who hears and acts is like a prudent builder who "dug deeply and laid the foundation on rock; when a flood arose, the river burst against that house but could not shake it, because it had been well built" (Lk 6:48–49). Mother Teresa commented:

> Those who see us must see
> the love of Jesus.... The God
> we are to reveal is the God who
> first revealed Himself as love.
> It is love that must direct every
> decision and every action.

It grieved Mother Teresa that young people today often lack the opportunity to see God in the adult Christians who surround them. Although they hear many fine words from preachers, teachers, and others, they observe that "They say one thing, but they do another." Vocations do not take root in the rocky ground that lacks genuine witness to Christ. Mother Teresa reminds us:

> Nowadays especially,
> young people want to see.
> You speak of love,
> you speak of prayer;

> they want to know how you love
> and how you pray and what
> "compassion" means for you.
> And on this they judge,
> how you really live the life …
> as a carrier of the love of God.

The young need to see in adults the unshakeable conviction that nothing can separate them from the love of Christ who calls them into full friendship with him. They must witness to young people every day that love of God overflows into love for all — especially those deprived of family, home, health, or human dignity. Their example will guide seekers of every age to the one for whom they hunger. As Mother Teresa said:

> Let the people see that
> you are happy to be
> what you are, a Christian.
> I think that's our
> biggest responsibility.

Those who live in neighborhoods where people of many religions live side by side can enter together into ministry with the poor. Mother Teresa found that many Hindus, Muslims, and Buddhists chose to work with the Missionaries of Charity because they sensed the presence of God in the Sisters. Likewise, they knew that they would be free to serve God in their own way. The founder noted:

I want very much for people
to come to know God,
to love Him, to serve Him,
for that is true happiness.
And what I have I want
everyone in the world to have.
But it is their choice.

Mother Teresa regarded highly those called to share in the church's missionary labors. Like Jesus himself, they are "moved with pity" for the sick, the dying, the troubled, and the outcast. Missionaries, whether priests, religious, or laypersons, hear and take to heart the Master's complaint: "The harvest is plentiful, but the laborers are few" (Mt 9:37). Mother Teresa described their vocation in the following words:

A Missionary is one who is sent.
God sent His Son.
Today God sends us.
Each one of us is sent by God
and His Church.
Sent for what? …
Sent to bring His love and
compassion among men.
We have to carry Our Lord
to places He has not
walked before.

Although most are not full-time missionaries like Mother Teresa, every Christian is a full-time disciple called to make Christ present to those around them and to work toward the coming of God's kingdom on earth. By baptism, they have been clothed with Christ and commissioned to give witness to him in their daily lives. They are called to see in the least the Lord of all and to serve them with authentic Christian charity. Mother Teresa concludes:

> I pray very, very specially for each one of you that we together fulfill God's will in all things so that we can all look up and see only Jesus in the work that He has entrusted to us, and that the people can look up and see only Jesus in us.

Filled with the Holy Spirit

All of them were filled with the Holy Spirit and began to speak in other languages, as the Spirit gave them ability.

Acts 2:4

Jesus ... sent the Holy Spirit among His apostles, and He gave them the wonderful word, "Go." ... Go and preach the news that God is love, and God loves you. And today, you are being sent....

Mother Teresa

In Mother Teresa's energetic and unfailing love, people around the world sensed the presence of the Holy Spirit. She had to speak in only one language to be understood by Asians, Africans, Europeans, and Americans. Her life of service spoke the international language of love. Even in her last years, when a heart condition jeopardized her health, her vitality testified to the Spirit's presence within. The light in the eyes of this self-effacing Christian missionary drew believers and unbelievers alike.

Mother Teresa would turn praise of her as a woman filled with the Holy Spirit to another woman whom she referred to as a "true missionary."

> Mary was the first Missionary of
> Charity. After welcoming Jesus
> into her heart and into her womb,
> she rose and went in haste to
> bring Jesus to John and to do
> the humble work of a servant for
> her cousin Elizabeth.
> Jesus in her, came in contact with
> John and he leapt for joy in his
> mother's womb.

Mother Teresa would also be quick to point out that in the upper room with the apostles, Mary awaited the Advocate Christ promised. "All these were constantly devoting themselves to prayer, together with certain women, including

Mary the mother of Jesus, as well as his brothers"
(Acts 1:14). Mary too experienced the Pentecost
and participated in the life of the rapidly growing
early church. As Mother Teresa observed:

> For just as she helped Jesus to
> grow, so she also helped the
> Church to grow in the beginning.

At the Last Supper, when his friends began to
grieve at Jesus' impending departure, he promised
them an Advocate to teach and comfort them.
"When the Spirit of truth comes," Jesus said,
"he will guide you into all the truth" (Jn 16:13).
Mother Teresa reminds us that the same Spirit
of truth abides in each Christian and empowers
them to love as Jesus loved.

> The early Christians were
> recognized by their love for each
> other…. I think that they must
> have taken Jesus' words
> seriously, "By this shall all men
> know that you are my disciples,
> if you love one another."

Mother Teresa recognized that the renewal
the church and each of its members seeks is "an
interior, radical change of the human heart by the
grace of God." It is a renewal to be sought in
prayer and practiced in daily life. The Spirit comes
to the aid of our weakness; "for we do not know
how to pray as we ought" (Rm 8:26). This same

Holy Spirit prays in us and intercedes for us when we open our hearts to God. Mother Teresa points out:

> Who will teach you how to pray?
> The Holy Spirit. Invoke [Him]
> often, "Holy Spirit, teach me how
> to pray." It is through prayer that
> we get the grace of a deep faith
> and faith comes through prayer.

The sacrament of confirmation, sometimes called "a second baptism," confers strength in the Holy Spirit and the power to be a true witness of Christ. Jesus says today, as he did to his friends at the Last Supper: "But the Advocate, the Holy Spirit, whom the Father will send in my name, will teach you everything, and remind you of all that I have said to you" (Jn 14:26). Mother Teresa assures us:

> I pray for you that the Holy Spirit
> may fill you with His purity — so
> that you can see the face of God
> in each other and in the faces of
> the poor you serve.

Becoming One in the Church

That they may all be one. As you, Father, are in me and I am in you, may they also be in us, so that the world may believe that you have sent me.

John 17:21

The last prayer of Jesus is: "That they may be one".... Ask Jesus to make us one; let us be united in Jesus.

Mother Teresa

Mother Teresa and Chiara Lubich (1985)

Perhaps because her missionary work took her to countries far and wide, Mother Teresa realized the church's universality. Whether in Calcutta or Rome, Bangladesh or Brooklyn, she anticipated the same unity for which Jesus prayed at the Last Supper. This was not a surface uniformity of liturgical sameness, but a union of hearts and souls achieved through the Holy Spirit. As Paul wrote to the Corinthians: "In the one Spirit we were all baptized into one body — Jews or Greeks, slaves or free — and we were all made to drink of one Spirit" (1 Cor 12:13). And Mother Teresa observed:

As we find Jesus in the Eucharist and in His poor, we are also called to help others to find Him there. Our works of love have become a means of unity. If you come to Calcutta, you will see it so clearly. Many volunteers from different nations — Japanese, Indians, Australians, Europeans, Americans, come everyday to the Motherhouse for a little talk, Holy Mass and Holy Hour. Where they stay, they also pray together. It is so wonderful to see them working together at our different homes for the poor.... There many have touched and experienced God.

The leader of the Missionaries of Charity loved deeply and relied upon the church she had vowed to serve. She considered the church a mother who supported her at every moment. And she encouraged her Sisters and Brothers to be worthy daughters and sons of this loving mother. Mother Teresa observed:

> Jesus gave His Church all that
> is needed to build up the family
> — for He gave us Himself in
> His word, in His sacraments,
> and in His authority — and we
> find all these in His Church.
> Listening to His word, families
> hear Jesus the Truth.
> Obeying His commands,
> they follow Jesus the Way.
> Receiving His sacraments,
> they live in Jesus the Life.

Mother Teresa desired, worked for, and prayed for the unity of the church so that its witness to the world might more effectively draw people to Christ. She desired the same communion in Christ that she experienced with her Sisters and Brothers for all who follow him in their respective vocations. She appreciated the reality of the different gifts (prophecy, teaching, leading, guiding, giving charitable support, caring for the sick) that come from the same Spirit. She cherished Paul's conviction that "we, who are many, are one body in Christ, and individually we are members one of another" (Rom 12:5). Emphasizing the need for this unity, she said:

We are all brothers and sisters
to each other with God as our
Father. It doesn't matter whether
rich or poor, what job we have,
what color, religion, language,
caste or creed. To be able to see
each other like that, with the eyes
of God, we need prayer.
Prayer gives a clean heart,
and a clean heart can see
God in each person around us.
And if we can see God in our
neighbor, we will love Him and
want to serve Him in our family,
our neighbor, in that dying man,
that poor widow, that hungry
child.... Let us remember that
whatever we do to the least and
poorest we do to God Himself for
Jesus said, "Whatever you do to
the least, you do it to Me."

Mother Teresa knew well how the bad or even thoughtless example of even one Christian could remain in the memory as an obstacle to Christianity itself. Thus, she frequently called people back to prayer and gospel meditation as a means of returning to a faithful witness of Christ. The more authentically we represent Christ to others, the more "one and holy" our church becomes, and the more readily we become one with all humanity. Mother Teresa observed:

[T]he more we allow Christ to
live His life in our lives, the more
Christlike we become. His Father
seeing Him in us, we will be His
beloved child then. That's the
aim of our life ... we are here to
become that.

Because of their universal outreach and membership, the Missionaries of Charity feel a particular responsibility to maintain harmony with all people of faith, as well as with those who profess no faith. Ambassadors for Christ, they, like their founder, see him in every distressing disguise humanity can wear. As Mother Teresa said:

By our living and working
together as God's family,
we proclaim that unity in the
Church, as well as by working
with all people, serving
all people, of any religion,
color, caste or race.

Mother Teresa did not achieve this prized unity of life easily, nor will anyone else. Yet we know that with God's help it is possible when we unite ourselves with Jesus and work in his place in the world around us. As our co-workers, we count all who belong to the one, holy, catholic, and apostolic Church. Mother Teresa concludes:

If families come to be places of
love and peace and holiness,
then our nations and our world
will live in love, peace and union
with God and each other.

Living in the Peace of Christ

Blessed are the peacemakers, for they will be called children of God.

Matthew 5:9

All works of love are works of peace. And therefore today if we have no peace it is because we have forgotten that we belong to each other — that that man, that woman, that child is my brother or my sister.

Mother Teresa

Although Mother Teresa of Calcutta personifies the fifth of Jesus' beatitudes, "Blessed are the merciful," she likewise embodies the seventh: "Blessed are the peacemakers." The Pope John XXIII Peace Prize (1971), the Albert Schweitzer International Peace Prize (1975), and the Nobel Peace Prize (1979) honored her contributions to world peace. In Mother Teresa's "veneration for life" and deep respect for human dignity, the presenters of these prestigious awards recognized a model for international relations on every scale.

As the presenter of the Nobel Peace Prize put it: "On the international level our efforts can only serve the cause of peace if they do not offend the self-respect of the poor nations. All aid given by the rich countries must be given in the spirit of Mother Teresa." The recipient herself, who asked the assembly to join her in offering the Peace Prayer of Francis of Assisi, observed:

> And I think that we in our family,
> we don't need bombs and guns,
> to destroy to bring peace — just
> get together, love one another,
> bring that peace, that joy, that
> strength of presence of each
> other in the home. And we will be
> able to overcome all the evil that
> is in the world.

Mother Teresa accepted the Nobel Prize in the name of those she and her Missionaries of

Charity served daily — the homeless, the hungry, the outcasts, all those whom society shuns. With the Nobel Prize money she built a shelter for the homeless, saying:

> Because I believe that love begins at home, and if we can create a home for the poor — I think that more and more love will spread. And we will be able through this understanding love to bring peace, be the good news to the poor.

Throughout her ministry to the least, Mother Teresa emphasized the need to recognize their human dignity and what they contribute to those who give. She often held up the example of poor persons who willingly sacrificed what little they had to help others in the "throwaway society." A paralyzed man with a subsistence income gave Mother Teresa fifteen dollars he had saved by giving up smoking — his one enjoyment — for a week. She encouraged everyone, whatever their material resources, with these words:

> Let us make sacrifices. Let us allow God to love through us.

Because she saw Jesus in every single person she served, Mother Teresa also saw the connection between loving the poor and making peace in the world. When we love our neighbor as ourselves — especially the neighbor who is suffering

— we close the gaps between us and allow Jesus to "guide our feet into the path of peace" (Lk 1:79). Mother Teresa observed:

> [T]he service of the poor is not
> the end, the service of the poor is
> a means to put our love for Christ
> into action.
> That's why we owe the poor
> people tremendous gratitude,
> and that's why they are the hope
> of salvation for mankind.

Like Jesus himself weeping over Jerusalem ("If you, even you, had only recognized on this day the things that make for peace! But now they are hidden from your eyes" [Lk 19:42]), Mother Teresa deeply regretted the world's blindness to "the things that make for peace." In her Nobel Prize acceptance speech, she said:

> Many people are very, very
> concerned with children in India,
> with the children of Africa where
> quite a number die, maybe of
> malnutrition, of hunger and so
> on, but millions are dying
> deliberately by the will of the
> mother. And this is what is the
> greatest destroyer of peace today.
> Because if a mother can kill her
> own child, what is left for me to

kill you and you to kill me?
There is nothing between.

Mother Teresa called on all nations to preach and practice the peace of Christ. She stressed the power of loving our neighbor, a power that would do away with the need for "tanks and generals" if it were practiced more faithfully. In a letter to President George Bush before the 1991 Gulf War, she wrote:

You have the power and
the strength to destroy God's
presence and image, His men,
His women, and His children.
Please listen to the will of God.
God has created us to be loved by
His love and not to be destroyed
by our hatred.... Please choose
the way of peace.... You may win
the war but what will the cost
be on people who are broken,
disabled and lost?

As a disciple of the Prince of Peace, Mother Teresa prayed that the entire world would come to experience the harmony and unity of God's kingdom. She was one with the incarnate Lord who came into the world bearing peace and with the risen Lord who greeted his followers, "Peace be with you." As she said:

> Let us radiate the peace
> of God and so light His light and
> extinguish in the world and in the
> hearts of all men all hatred and
> love for power.

The modest religious woman who won three international peace prizes sought no fame or glory for her work among the poorest of the poor. She did, however, desire that all Christians dedicate themselves to pursuing "what makes for peace and for mutual upbuilding" (Rom 14:19). Her counsel is simplicity itself:

> [W]hen you find Jesus you will
> find peace, love, unity.

Walking with Jesus Today

And remember, I am with you always,
to the end of the age.

Matthew 28:20

Our work is for today; yesterday
has gone, tomorrow has not yet
come ... we have only today to
make Jesus known, loved and
served.

Mother Teresa

The woman sometimes called "the saint of the gutters" attributed all that she was and all that she accomplished to God, the love of her life. Like St. Thérèse of Lisieux, Mother Teresa understood the meaning of "The Eternal Today." As Thérèse observed in her poem of that title: "You know, O my God, / That to love you here on earth — / I have only today." The present moment is always the time in which to walk with Jesus and deepen our friendship with him.

> You must have that intimate
> relationship with Jesus. "Jesus in
> my heart, I believe in Your tender
> love for me. I love You." Say this
> often. Make it a part of you. You
> must know Jesus to love Him.

Just as the first disciples walked side by side with the Master who had called "Follow me," Mother Teresa remained in his company through her childhood, her first vocation as a teaching Sister, and her second vocation as the servant of the least. She held nothing back. Her daily prayer was:

> Dear Jesus, help me to spread
> Thy fragrance everywhere I go.
> Flood my soul with Thy spirit
> and life. Penetrate and possess
> my whole being so utterly that all
> my life may only be a radiance of
> Thine. Shine through me, and be

so in me that every soul
I come in contact with may feel
Thy presence in my soul.
Let them look up and see no
longer me but only Jesus....

From around the world people came to ask Mother Teresa how they could assist in her missionary work. If they expected an easy answer, they never received one. Loving as Jesus loved required more than a donation of surplus, more than a willingness to work for a time among the poor in a faraway land. Mother Teresa's instruction awakened many from their idealistic vision of themselves as missionaries:

It hurt Jesus to love us; it hurt
God to love us because He had
to give. He gave His Son. Today
... what I want from you is that
we look together and we see the
poor in our own family, that we
begin at home to love until it
hurts, that we have a ready smile,
that we have time for our people.
If we know our people then we
will know who is our next door
neighbor.... Do we know the
people around us?

She wanted Christians to recognize that walking by faith and staying the course required a firm commitment to unselfish love. Yet when

Part 3: To Bear Witness

she sensed that others needed encouragement in their attempts to minister to their own families and neighborhoods, she readily complied. As she said:

> Each time anyone comes
> in contact with us, they must
> become different and better
> people because of having met us.
> We must radiate God's love.

Mother Teresa had a special sensitivity to the sick who feel relegated to the sidelines of active Christian life. Many wished that they could serve God by volunteering at soup kitchens or thrift shops, helping out in the parish or the local community. They needed to hear a maternal voice assuring them of their indispensable contribution to the body of Christ.

> In addition to your prayers and
> sacrifices, my Sick and
> Suffering Co-Workers, your
> sufferings accepted in love with
> Jesus are the source of many
> graces. You are sharing
> wholeheartedly in all that we do.

The willing acceptance of suffering was, for Mother Teresa, a crucial identification with Jesus. Whatever the illness, disability, addiction, or deprivation, the one who carried it with faith was, to her mind, a clear reflection of Christ himself. The goodness of one who suffers well can readily call others to conversion and gratitude for their own blessings. Mother Teresa reflected:

> I think only holiness will be able
> to overcome evil and overcome
> all the sufferings and miseries
> of the people, and of our own life
> also because we too have to
> suffer and suffering is a gift of
> God if we use it in the right way.
> The cross must be there and so
> let us thank God for this.

For those whose faith walk takes them daily to the sickroom or the shelter, the hospital or the nursing home, Mother Teresa had an abiding love. She suffered a heart attack and received a pacemaker. A respiratory ailment kept her from doing the work she loved. From her own experience, she could see Christ in both the caregiver and the care receiver. She observed:

> Your hands are feeding the hungry
> Christ, your hands are clothing
> the naked Christ, your hands are
> giving home to the homeless
> Christ in some part of the work.
> So, do your work well, and do
> it with great love. Otherwise it is
> not worth doing it.... That is the
> means for you to become holy
> because Jesus our God is there.

During her hospitalization in 1989, Mother Teresa spoke with her countryman Fr. Lush Gjergji about her dream of "bringing Jesus to Albania." Even in her illness she was writing letters and telegrams, paving the way for the Missionaries of Charity in the land of her ancestors. Despite numerous obstacles, Mother Teresa's vision of many missionary houses and vocations soon became a reality. As she confided to Fr. Gjergji:

> Only now do I understand the reason for my illness, and I am quite content. See, I am in good company with Jesus. All for Jesus.

Afterword

On World Mission Sunday, October 19, 2003, John Paul II presided over the beatification of Mother Teresa of Calcutta. Shortly after her death on September 5, 1997, the cause for her canonization was begun, a dispensation of the usual five-year waiting period having been granted. Mother Teresa's holiness shone so brightly that no one doubted her eventual formal recognition as a saint of the Roman Catholic Church.

In his homily, John Paul II reminded the congregation at Saint Peter's that Mother Teresa had chosen to be the servant to the least. "Her life was a radical living and a bold proclamation of the gospel," he observed. The Holy Father recalled the ways in which she had been a sign of God's love, presence, and compassion to all in need. He repeated her insight that "the greatest poverty is to be unwanted." And he praised her as "a humble Gospel messenger and a tireless benefactor of humanity."

Blessed Mother Teresa of Calcutta, who began her religious life as a "shy, quiet, and ordinary" novice of the Sisters of Loreto, became one of the greatest missionaries of the twentieth century.

If her words had never been recorded, her accomplishments alone would be inspiration enough. Like Francis of Assisi, she understood the advice, "Preach the gospel always. If necessary, use words." Her holiness lies primarily in her actions. In her life of service, we see the meaning of Jesus' washing the disciples' feet at the Last Supper. We see one who embodied Christ's teaching: "Whoever wishes to be first among you will be slave of all" (Mk 10:44).

Throughout this book, we have directed our attention to the word of the Lord and the words of Mother Teresa. We have reflected on how to integrate her example of living, loving, and giving witness in our own circumstances. Should we need an image to hold in our hearts we can picture her holding a child, a vagrant, or a dying person with one hand and with the other fingering her rosary.

Having come full circle with Blessed Mother Teresa, we return to ponder her opening words:

> **Life is the most beautiful gift of God. He has created us in His image, for greater things: to love and to be loved.**